Terrific Shoes

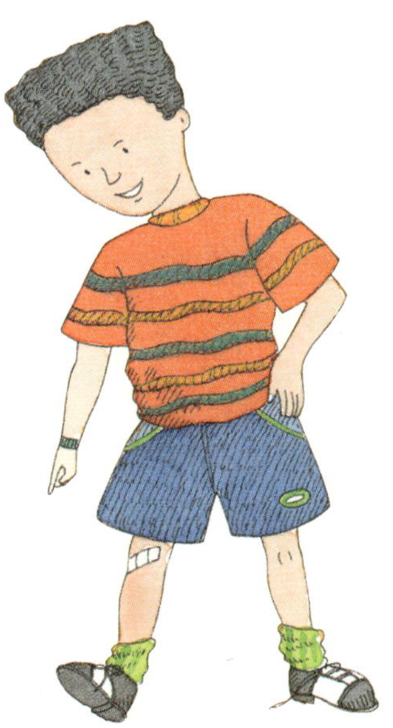

Written by Anne Miranda

Illustrated by Jessica Clerk

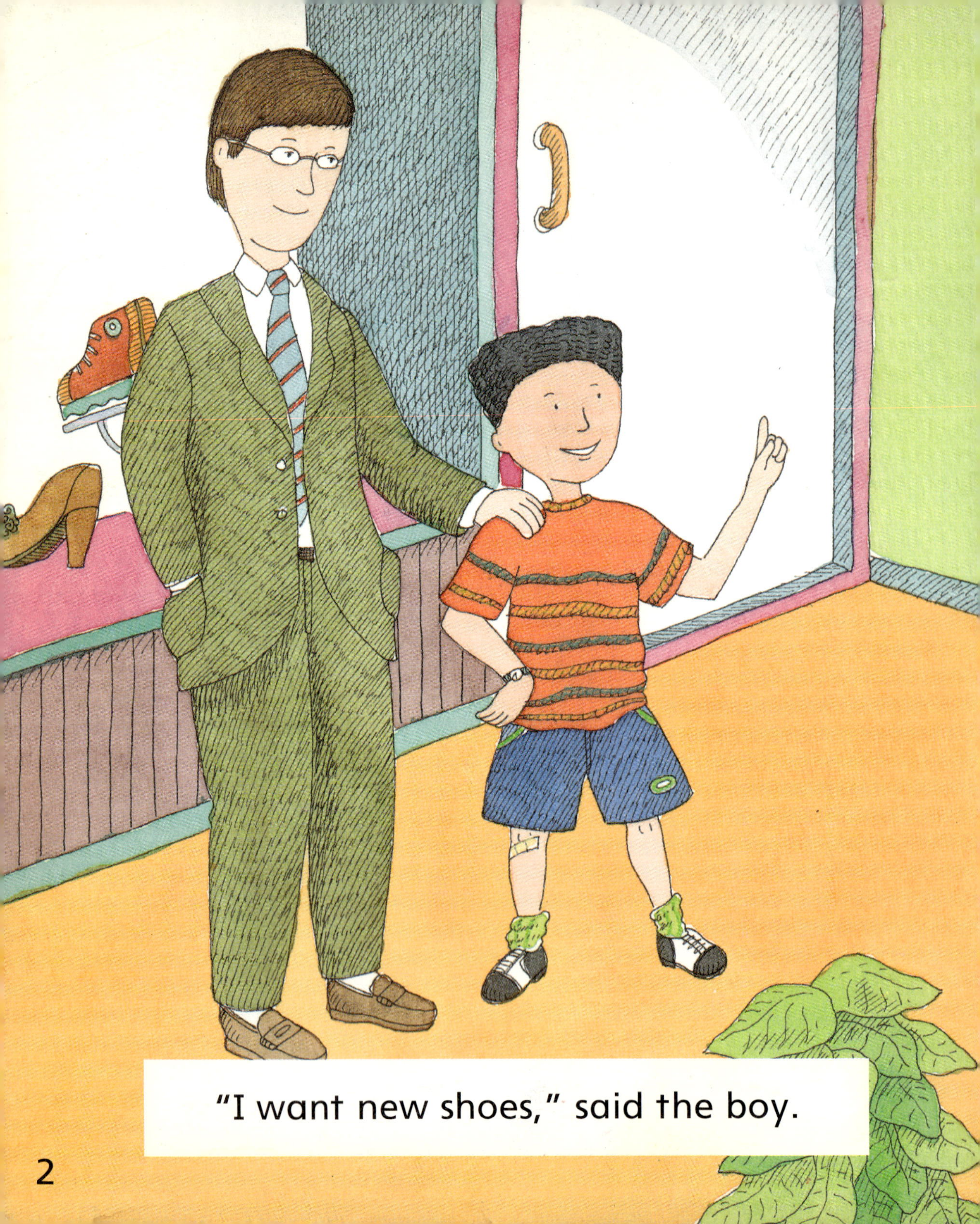

"I want new shoes," said the boy.

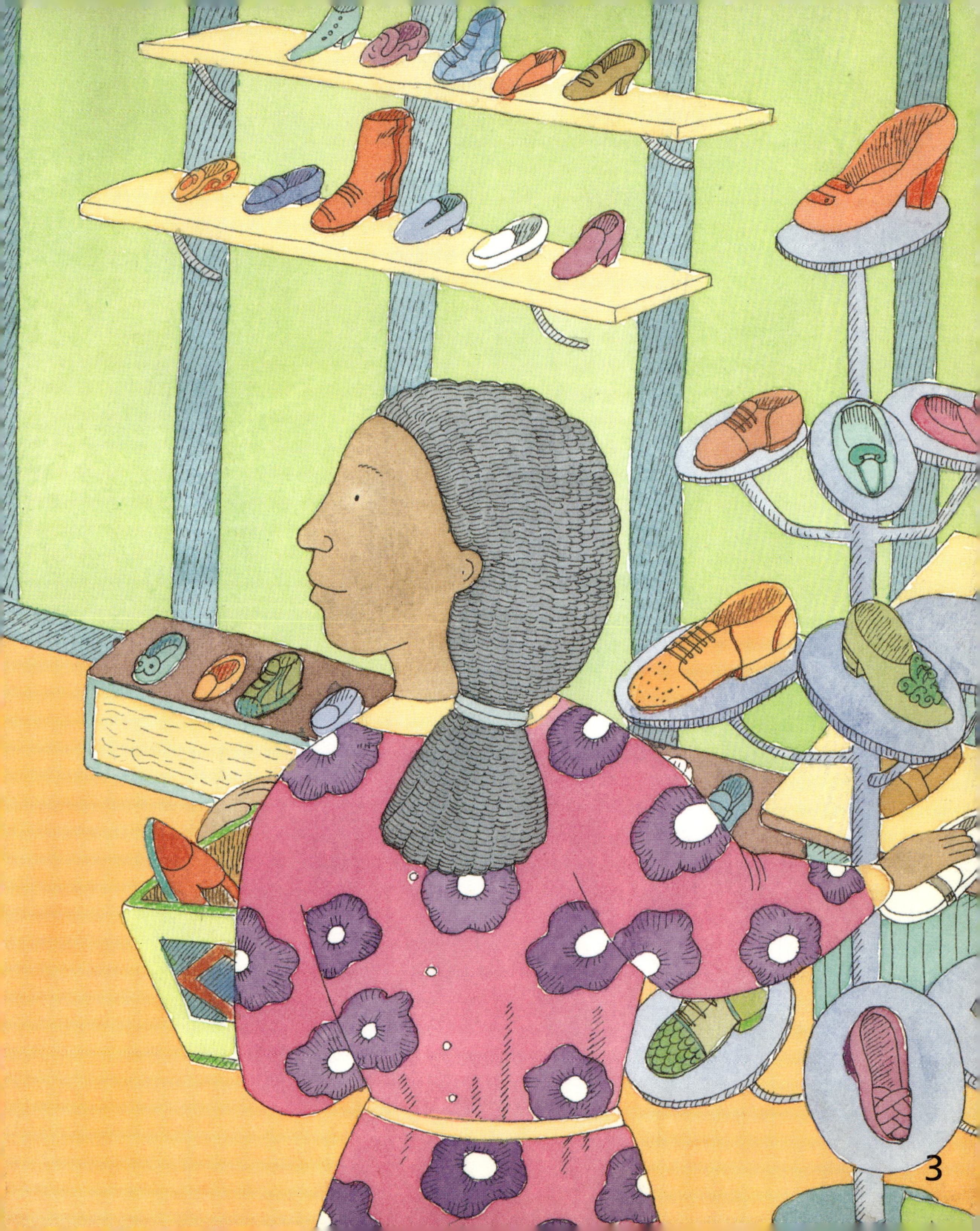

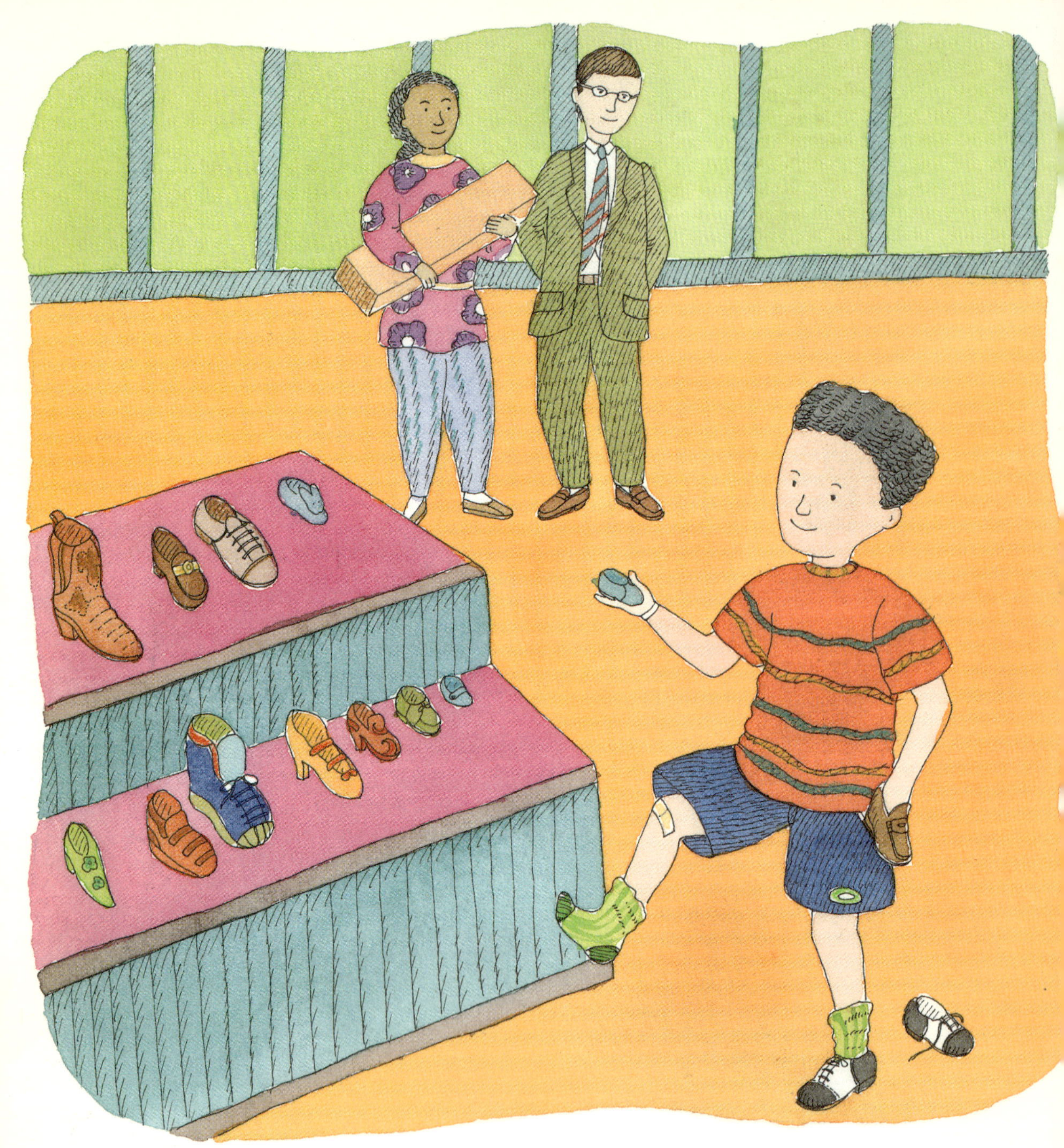

Too tiny...

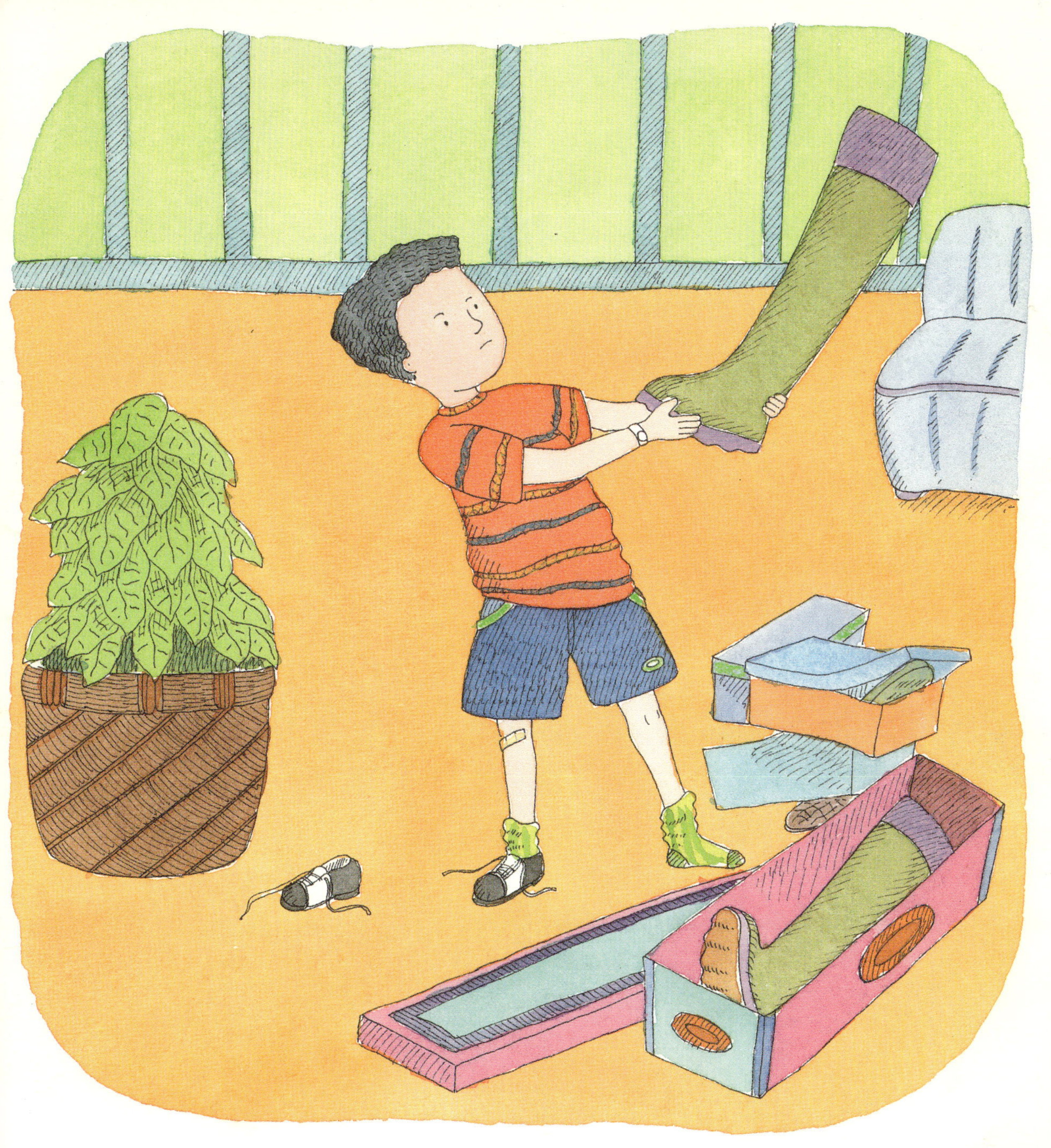

Too tall...

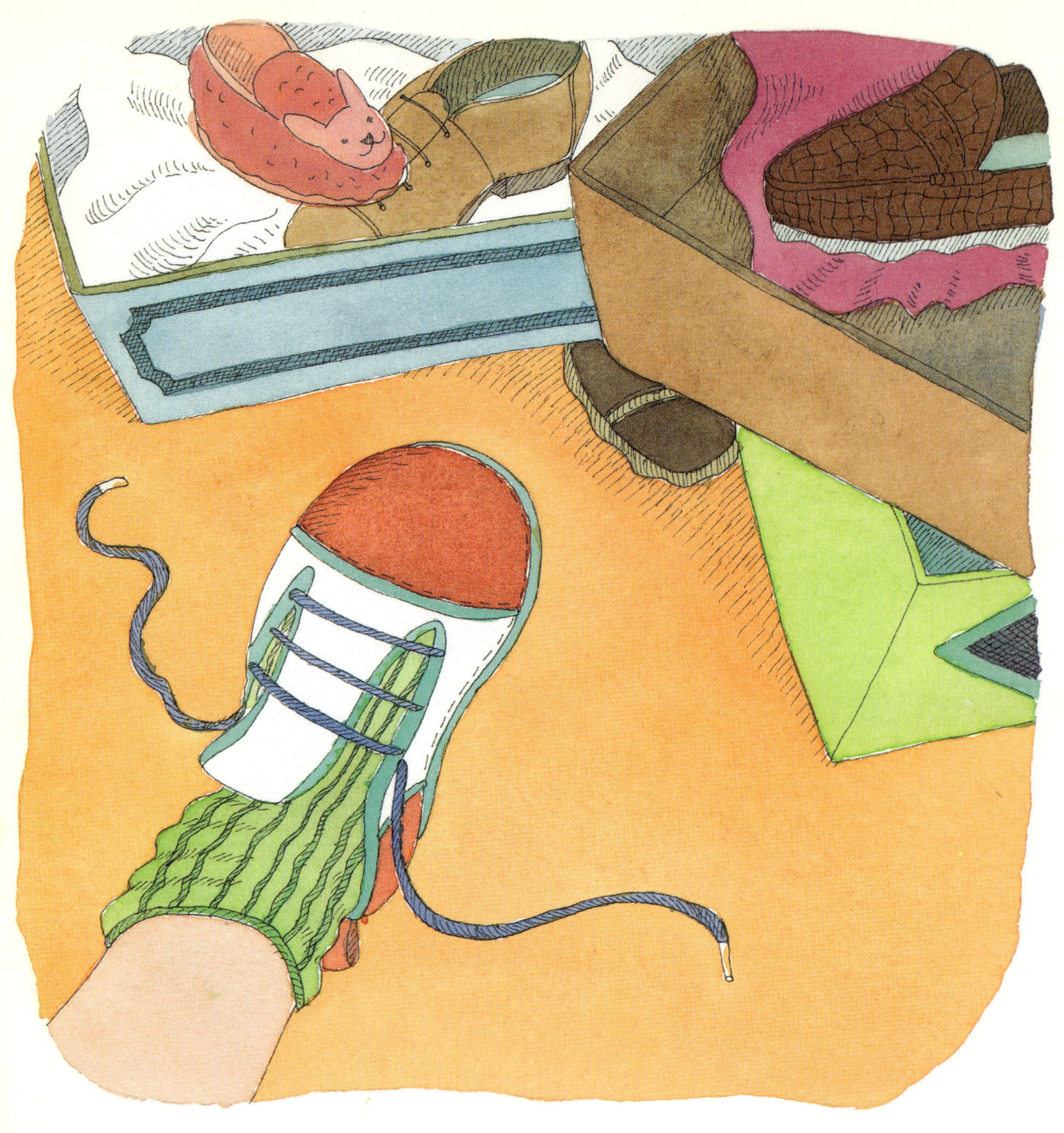

Too tight...

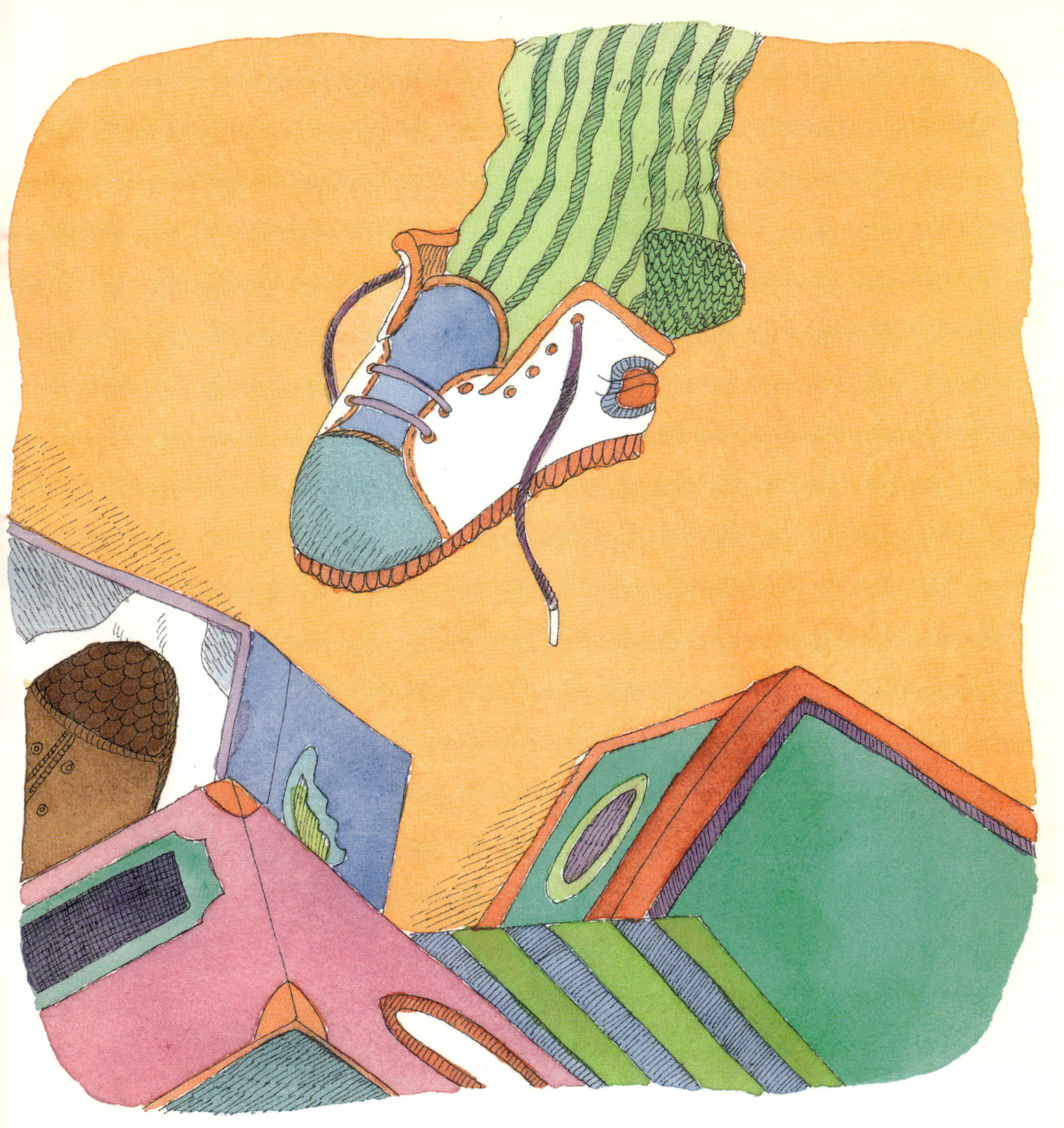

Too small...

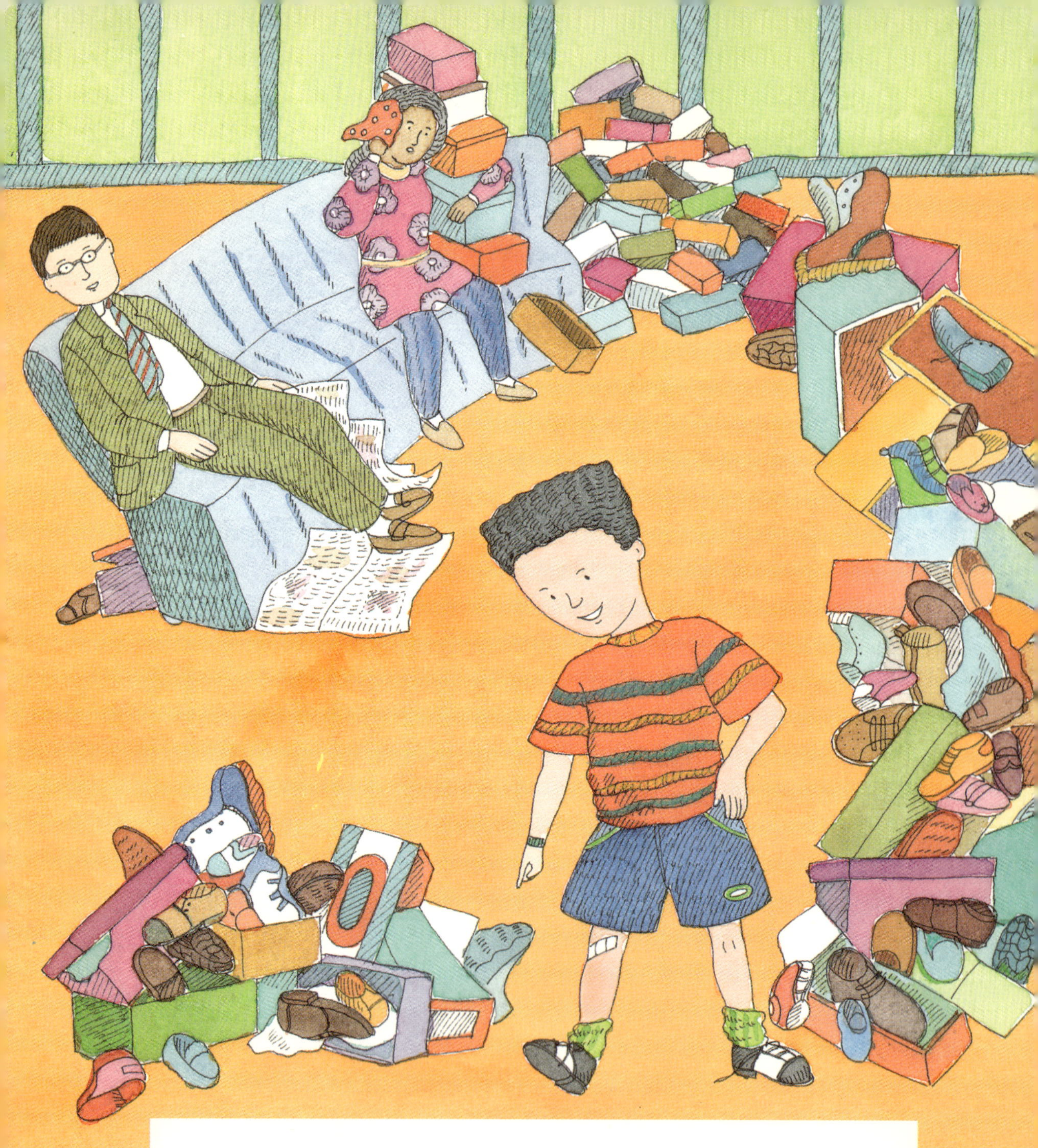

"Terrific!" said the boy.